D1422749

THE
ABC
OF
DESSERTS

WITH DECORATIONS BY
RUTH McCREA

THE PETER PAUPER PRESS
MOUNT VERNON · NEW YORK

COPYRIGHT 1958 • THE PETER PAUPER PRESS

DEAR READER:

The good hostess likes to have every course a good one. But the dessert, which comes to the table last, and stays longest in the memory, is of particular importance. And while there *is* a school of gourmets that fancies fruit and cheese above all else, the recipes on the following pages are for the sweeter of tooth!

If you are both cook and hostess, and want last-minute freedom to enjoy the company, I heartily recommend the many desserts that may be prepared the day before and set in the refrigerator until the last minute: the various ice-box cakes, Surprise Pie, and my own favorite Carrot Cake, which is not a frozen dessert, but can easily be made the day before.

And for real parties, remember that whipped cream and icings, when squeezed through a pastry tube, give a professional air to your home-made pies and cakes.

THE EDITOR

*pple's the fruit,
To tempt any guy;
In pudding or dumpling,
Brown Betty or pie!*

APPLE-ALMOND PUDDING

3 pounds tart apples
Granulated sugar (to sweeten apples)
1/4 pound whole almonds, ground
3 egg yolks
1/2 cup sugar
1 lemon (grated rind and juice)
3 egg whites

Peel and core apples, and cut into eighths.
Butter glass baking dish, and arrange
apples in it. Sprinkle apples with sugar,
and bake until tender. Beat egg yolks with
1/2 cup sugar. Add ground nuts, lemon
juice and rind. Fold in egg whites, which

5

have been beaten stiff. Pour batter over apples and bake ½ hour in a 325° oven.

ALMOND TORTE

4 cups fine sugar
4 cups almonds, chopped very fine
10 eggs, separated
2 tablespoons light cream
Cocoa
¼ slice citron

Mix sugar and almonds, add yolks, light cream and egg whites, stiffly beaten.

Spread half the mixture in round buttered cake form, sift the cocoa on it, about ⅛ inch thick, distribute the finely cut citron evenly and then top with the remaining mixture. Bake in 350° oven until done. Serve hot or cold with rum-flavored whipped cream.

APRICOT CREAM PIE

1 pound dried apricots
½ cup sugar
3 egg whites
½ pint sweet cream
1 baked 9-inch pie shell

Stew the dried apricots, which have been

6

allowed to soak a few hours, in enough water to cover, adding sugar. When soft, strain, allowing some of the syrup to moisten the strained apricots. Beat egg whites until stiff, and fold into the apricot mixture. Pour into a bottom crust which has been baked beforehand, and allow pie to set for 15 minutes in a 350° oven. Cover with whipped cream when ready to serve.

APPLE SPONGE CAKE

3 eggs, separated
¾ cup sugar
1 cup toasted cake crumbs or lady fingers
½ cup almonds, blanched
4 apples, peeled and grated
½ lemon (juice and grated peel)

Separate eggs. To the yolks, add sugar, grated apples, toasted cake crumbs, lemon juice and rind. Fold in beaten egg whites gently. Pour batter into greased spring form, sprinkle almonds on top. Bake in a 350° oven for 25 minutes, or until done.

Garnish with whipped cream around the top edge of the cake. Fresh strawberries, glazed with raspberry jam, melted, may be used to cover the middle area, inside the circle of whipped cream.

Blueberry cake
Is a real special treat,
When served up with cream,
And not made too sweet!

BLUEBERRY APPLE CRISP

3 cups blueberries
3 cups tart apples, sliced
Brown sugar, to taste
1 cup flour
¾ cup sugar
1 teaspoon baking powder
¾ teaspoon salt
1 egg
⅓ cup butter, melted
½ teaspoon cinnamon

Grease baking dish and add apples and blueberries, brown sugar to taste. Mix flour, sugar, baking powder, salt and unbeaten egg with fork until mixture be-

8

comes crumbly. Sprinkle over fruit. Top with cooled, melted butter and sprinkle with cinnamon. Bake at 350° ½ hour or until top is golden brown. Serve warm with cream. Serves 6-8.

Peaches may be substituted for berries.

BLUEBERRY CAKE

¼ pound butter
1 cup sugar
2 eggs, separated
1½ cups flour
⅓ cup milk
1 teaspoon baking powder
¼ teaspoon salt
1½ cups blueberries
1 teaspoon vanilla

Cream butter, add sugar, and blend together. Beat yolks of eggs well and add to first mixture. Sift flour, baking powder and salt together and add alternately with the milk. Then fold in the stiffly beaten egg whites and vanilla. Pour ½ of the batter into a well-greased oblong pan, cover with the blueberries and then with the remaining batter. Bake in 350° oven, for 35 minutes. Sprinkle with powdered sugar. Serve hot.

BABA AU RHUM

Baba Cakes

4 eggs
1/2 cup granulated sugar
1 1/4 cups sifted flour
4 teaspoons baking powder
6 tablespoons butter, melted
1/2 cup lukewarm milk

Beat eggs with sugar until fluffy; add flour and baking powder, sifted together. Mix; then add butter and milk. Mix vigorously. Pour into a buttered and floured pudding mold or individual molds. Bake individual molds 25 minutes or a large mold 35 to 40 minutes, at 325°. Remove from oven; unmold; and while still hot pour rum syrup over the baba. Cool and serve with sweetened whipped cream with a dash of rum flavor.

Rum Syrup

1/2 cup granulated sugar
1/2 cup water
1/2 cup rum

Cook sugar in water until a thin syrup is formed. Remove from heat and add rum. 8 servings.

10

BLACK BOTTOM PIE

1 envelope gelatine
¾ cup sugar
⅛ teaspoon salt
1 egg yolk, slightly beaten
¾ cup milk
4 squares unsweetened chocolate
1 cup icy cold evaporated milk, whipped
1 teaspoon vanilla
1 baked 9-inch pie shell
1 cup cream, whipped and sweetened

Mix gelatine, sugar, and salt in top of double boiler. Combine egg yolk and milk and add to gelatine mixture. Add 3 squares of the chocolate. Cook over boiling water until chocolate is melted, stirring often. Remove from heat and beat with egg beater until smooth. Chill until thickened. Then fold in whipped evaporated milk and vanilla. Pile into pie shell and chill.

Spread with whipped cream. Shave remaining 1 square chocolate into long curls with vegetable slicer. Sprinkle over pie.

A taste of the Old South!

Chocolate's the flavor
For cake in our house;
There's never a crumb
Left over for Mickey the Mouse!

CARROT CAKE DE-LUXE

1 cup carrot pulp
5 eggs, separated
1 cup sugar
1 teaspoon vanilla
1 cup walnuts, chopped
1 pinch salt
½ pint cream, whipped

Cook and strain carrots; squeeze dry. Mix egg yolks, sugar and salt and beat lightly. Stir in carrot pulp and fold in stiffly beaten egg whites. Add chopped nuts and vanilla. Bake in spring form for 45 minutes in a 400° oven. Cool. Serve with whipped cream.

cake;

y to bake!

PIE

elted
up
n well
ns
ed pie shell

sugar, syrup and butter, add eggs and cans. Fill unbaked pie shell with mixture and bake for 10 minutes at 400°, then for 30 to 35 minutes at 350°. Serve either cold or hot, with unsweetened whipped cream.

Quick and easy!

16

COFFEE JELLY PARFAIT

1 tablespoon unflavored gelatine, softened in
  ¼ cup cold water
1½ tablespoons instant coffee
2 cups water
⅓ cup sugar
1 tablespoon brandy (or brandy flavoring)
1 cup heavy cream
½ cup toasted almonds, chopped and salted

Heat 2 cups of water to boiling point. Add instant coffee, softened gelatine, sugar and stir until gelatine dissolves. Add flavoring and pour into a shallow pan to depth of about ½ inch. Chill until firm. Cut into ½-inch cubes.

Whip cream and sweeten to taste, then arrange alternate layers of coffee-jelly cubes, whipped cream and almonds in parfait glasses. Serves 6.

COFFEE PARFAIT

⅓ cup sugar
½ cup strong coffee
2 egg whites, stiffly beaten
1 pint cream, whipped

Combine sugar and coffee in saucepan. Cook over medium heat, stirring con-

13

stantly, until sugar is dissolved. Then boil without stirring until the syru~ ~nins a thread (238°).

Gradually add the hot syru~ stream, to the beaten egg whi~ constantly until the mixture ~ further.

Fold into above mixture. P~ ing tray and freeze until fir~ overnight. Serves 6-8.

COFFEE GELATIN~

1 package gelatine
1½ cups coffee (extra stro~
½ cup milk
1 cup sugar
4 eggs, separated
1 teaspoon vanilla
½ pint cream, whipped

Dissolve gelatine in c~ and beat yolks until ligh~ to gelatine and coffee. Add milk and ~ug~ slowly, stirring constantly, until mixture boils. Fold in stiffly beaten egg whites. Cool. Pour into wet mold and refrigerate. Serve with slightly sweetened whipped cream. Serves 6.

14

e-luxe is the word
For a creamy chees~
Easy to eat,
Though tric~

DIXIE PECAN

1 cup sugar
¼ cup butter, ~
½ cup corn sy~
3 eggs, beate~
1 cup pec~
1 unba~

Mi~
Pe~

Melt choco~ and thin out with bo~ gradually. Set over direct heat, and ~i~ to a boil, stirring constantly.

15

egg-nog in punch,
Egg-nog in pie,
The taste is the same —
Here's rum in your eye!

EGG NOG PIE

3 egg yolks, beaten
1/2 cup sugar
2 cups light cream
1/8 teaspoon salt
1/8 teaspoon nutmeg
Rum to taste
3 egg whites, stiffly beaten
1/2 recipe pastry

Beat egg yolks, sugar, and cream. Add salt, nutmeg, and rum. Fold in egg whites. Pour into 9-inch pastry-lined pie pan. Bake in 450° oven 10 minutes, then in 325° oven until firm, about 25 minutes. Top with whipped cream.

EAST INDIA PIE

1 unbaked pastry shell
2 egg yolks
1 cup sugar
1 teaspoon cinnamon
1 teaspoon cloves
½ cup pecan halves
½ cup seedless raisins
1 tablespoon melted butter
2 egg whites
1 tablespoon vinegar
½ pint cream, whipped

Beat egg yolks well until light and thick. Add gradually sugar which has been sifted with cinnamon and cloves. Then add pecan halves, seedless raisins and melted butter. Beat the egg whites until stiff but not dry, and fold them gently into the sugar mixture. Do not beat in. As you fold them in, add vinegar.

Pour into an 8-inch unbaked pastry shell. Bake in a hot oven, 450°, for 10 minutes. Then reduce the heat to 350° and bake 25 minutes more. Cool and serve with unsweetened whipped cream. Serves 6.

This recipe was brought back from India, and can be used at the end of an elegant meal!

ENGLISH MINCE PIES

1 pound finely chopped suet
1 pound currants
1 pound seedless raisins
½ pound bleached raisins
1 pound chopped apples
¼ pound mixed candied citron
1 pound superfine sugar
2 ounces brandy
½ teaspoon each mace, nutmeg, cinnamon
Juice of ½ lemon
Prepared pastry

Combine ingredients (except pastry) press into jars, and cover closely. Store in cool dry place for 3 or 4 weeks before using. (This recipe makes 4-5 lbs. of delicious mincemeat).

Tarts: Using a cookie cutter, cut 24 circles from prepared pastry dough. Line the 12 holes of a patty pan or muffin pan. Prick bottom of each with a fork to prevent rising. Put in 2 generous teaspoons of mincemeat. Cover with other circles, pinching around the edge to hold. Bake. Serve hot, dredged with fine sugar.

The aroma of baking mince pies in the kitchen gives a holiday atmosphere to the whole house!

rench pastry and tartlets
all running with goo,
Will win the young heart
Of the girl that you woo!

FRENCH PANCAKES

1½ cups sifted flour
1 teaspoon salt
1 tablespoon sugar
3 eggs, well-beaten
3 cups milk
3 tablespoons butter, melted
Tart jelly

Sift dry ingredients together into bowl.
Add milk and melted butter to beaten
eggs. Pour into flour mixture and stir until blended. Pour about ½ cup batter onto hot greased griddle. Turn over when
delicately brown and bake the other side.
Stack the baked pancakes in layers spread-
ing each layer with tart jelly. Serves 6.

raham-cracker cake,
With cream in between,
Flavored with orange,
Is fit for a queen!

GRAHAM CRACKER CAKE

½ cup shortening
1 cup sugar
3 eggs, separated
1 cup milk
2 dozen graham crackers
2 teaspoons baking powder
1 cup chopped nuts
½ teaspoon salt

Cream shortening and sugar together. Beat egg yolks until light and add. Then add milk. Roll crackers fine. Combine baking powder and salt with crumbs and add to first mixture together with chopped nuts. Lastly, cut in egg whites which

21

have been stiffly beaten. Bake 35-40 minutes in a 375° oven in greased layer pans. Top and fill with whipped cream.

GOURMET'S FUDGE CAKE

2 cups sifted flour
2 teaspoons baking powder
1/2 teaspoon soda
1/4 teaspoon salt
1/2 cup butter
1 cup sugar
2 egg yolks, well beaten
3 squares chocolate, melted
1 1/4 cups milk
1 teaspoon vanilla
2 egg whites, stiffly beaten

Sift flour once, measure, add baking powder, soda, and salt, and sift together 3 times. Cream butter thoroughly, add sugar gradually, and cream together until light and fluffy. Add egg yolks and chocolate; then flour, alternately with milk, a small amount at a time. Beat smooth after each addition. Add vanilla. Fold in whites.

Bake in 2 greased 9-inch layer pans in moderate oven, 350°, 30 minutes. Put layers together and when cool cover with your favorite chocolate frosting.

22

GRAPEFRUIT, BROILED

Cut grapefruit in half, crosswise; core and loosen the fruit. Serrate the edge of the skin with a sharp knife. Sprinkle well with granulated sugar and sherry, and let stand a few hours. When ready to serve, sprinkle with brown sugar, and broil for about 10 minutes, or until the grapefruit is hot through and through, and the top is golden brown. Serve with a maraschino cherry in the center.

GERMAN "ROTE GRUTZE"

1 ten-ounce package frozen raspberries
2 cups water
⅔ cup currant jelly
½ cup quick-cooking tapioca

In a saucepan, bring defrosted raspberries, 1½ cups water, and jelly to a boil. Add tapioca to remaining ½ cup of water, stirring to mix, then add gradually to boiling fruit in saucepan. Cook 1 minute, stirring constantly. Pour pudding into bowl. Stir every few minutes until cool. Refrigerate. Serves 4-6.

This is a shortened version of a favorite old-time dessert!

oliday Yeast Cake,
Filled with raisins and nuts—
Bake it today—
No ifs and no buts!

HOLIDAY YEAST CAKE

½ pound butter
2 tablespoons sugar
Pinch of salt
3 egg yolks
1 envelope yeast, dissolved in
  ¼ cup water
¼ cup milk
2½ cups flour, sifted
3 egg whites
1 cup sugar
1 cup walnut meats, broken
½ cup raisins
Cinnamon

Cream the butter, add sugar and a pinch
of salt. Separate eggs, and add the yolks

24

which have been beaten until light in color. Then the yeast which has been dissolved in luke-warm water, 1/4 cup milk, and the sifted flour. Roll into a ball and wrap in wax paper. Refrigerate overnight.

Next day. Beat the egg whites until stiff, folding in 1 cup sugar when eggs are beaten. Remove dough from refrigerator and separate into four parts, rolling each part into a rectangle about 8 x 16 inches. Spread egg whites onto the dough, and sprinkle with walnuts, raisins and cinnamon. Roll as for a jelly roll, and place the four rolls on a baking sheet, cut side down. Allow to rise for 1 hour in a warm place. Bake at 325° for 25 minutes. Cool, and sprinkle with confectioners' sugar.

HAWAIIAN PINEAPPLE MOUSSE

1 can crushed pineapple (20 oz.)
1 1/2 pints heavy cream, whipped
1 teaspoon lemon juice

Drain the crushed pineapple and fold carefully into whipped cream. Add lemon juice, cover and freeze in refrigerator overnight. Do not stir. Serves 10.

HOT POLICHINKAS

2 egg yolks
2 tablespoons sugar
Pinch of salt
1 cup sifted flour
¾ cup milk
2 egg whites
Apricot jam
Powdered sugar

Beat together egg yolks, sugar, and salt. Add flour and milk and beat until smooth. Beat egg whites stiff and fold in. Batter should be thin. Pour on hot greased griddle, tipping so that batter will spread over bottom. Brown one side and turn and brown the other. When done, spread with a thick apricot jam or any other desired jam. Roll up and sprinkle with powdered sugar.

HOT SPICY BAKED APPLES

6 baking apples
1½ cups mincemeat
⅓ cup brown sugar
¾ cup white wine
2 tablespoons sugar

Wash and core apples; peel off about ¼

of the peel and set the apples in a shallow baking dish. Fill each apple with 2 tablespoons of mincemeat. Sprinkle tops with brown sugar, spoon about half the wine over apples and bake for 40 minutes in a 350° oven or until apples are tender. Transfer hot apples to a hot serving plate. Stir remaining mincemeat and wine in the apple syrup and cook 10 minutes longer. Pour syrup over apples, sprinkle with granulated sugar and serve. Serves 6.

HAZELNUT TORTE

Layers
½ pound hazelnuts
¼ pound sugar
8 egg whites

Crisp nuts in oven then grind finely. Mix with sugar and whites. Bake in 3 layers in buttered tins at 400° for 20 minutes.

Filling
8 yolks
8 tablespoons sugar
3 bars sweet chocolate, melted
½ pound butter, creamed

Mix yolks, sugar, chocolate and butter thoroughly. Fill layers; cover top.

Imperial Rice
Made with cherries and liquor—
Use the quick-cooking kind—
It's smoother and slicker!

ICE-BOX CAKE [CHOCOLATE]

24 lady fingers
8 eggs, separated
½ pound chocolate bits, melted with
   3 tablespoons water
1 teaspoon instant coffee powder
1 teaspoon vanilla
½ pint cream, whipped

Melt chocolate in 3 tablespoons water; add instant coffee and vanilla. Add egg yolks one at a time, beating well. Fold in egg whites, stiffly beaten.

Line mold with lady fingers; pour in mixture. Refrigerate overnight. Serve topped with whipped cream. Serves 12.

28

*Jellies and jams,
when applied to a tart,
add spice to the cookie
and look very smart!*

JELLY ROLL

¾ cup sifted cake flour
¾ teaspoon baking powder
¼ teaspoon salt
4 eggs
¾ cup sugar
1 teaspoon vanilla
1 cup jelly, preferably tart

Start your oven at 400° and grease a 15"
x 10" x 1½" jelly-roll pan with shortening. Fit in layer of waxed paper neatly.
Sift and measure the flour accurately.

Mix baking powder, salt and eggs in a
large mixing bowl and beat until they be-
gin to thicken. Now add the sugar a little

at a time, beating constantly until the mixture is smooth. Add flour and vanilla, mixing them in with a gentle, folding motion. Pour batter into pan and bake 13 to 15 minutes.

While cake bakes, sprinkle a clean tea towel with a generous coating of confectioners' sugar. When your cake is finished, turn it out on the towel, peel off the waxed paper and roll towel, sugar and all up tightly. Cool roll 10 minutes, unroll carefully and spread with jelly. Roll again, wrap in towel and cool on rack.

JENNY'S CHEESECAKE

1 box zwieback
¼ cup butter
¾ cup sugar
1 teaspoon cinnamon
2 envelopes gelatine
1 cup cold water
3 egg yolks
1 pound cream cheese
Grated rind of 1 lemon
1 teaspoon lemon juice
1 cup heavy cream, lightly beaten
4 egg whites, stiffly beaten

Roll out zwieback to make fine crumbs

30

and mix with the butter, 1/4 cup of the sugar and cinnamon. Reserve 1/4 of the crumbs and press remainder firmly against the bottom and sides of a well-buttered 9-inch spring form pan. Bake for 10 minutes in a 400° oven.

Soak gelatine in 1/2 cup cold water for 5 minutes. Blend egg yolks, the remaining sugar and 1/2 cup water and cook, stirring constantly, over boiling water for 3 minutes. Add the gelatine and stir until it is thoroughly dissolved.

Gradually stir the cooked mixture into the cream cheese and strain through a fine sieve. Add the lemon rind and lemon juice. Fold in the whipped cream and egg whites until thoroughly blended. Pour into the prepared pan.

Sprinkle the remaining crumbs on top and chill in the refrigerator until set. Serves 8.

JIFFY FRUIT COMPOTE

Peel white grapes, dice a crisp apple, cut a ripe pineapple into chunks and combine with brandy and kirsch. Chill thoroughly before serving.

Katy, put the kettle on,
Kettle on, kettle on;
Katy, put the kettle on,
There's cake for our tea!

KIRSCH JELLY

1 cup boiling water
1 tablespoon gelatine, dissolved in
    ¼ cup water
¾ cup sugar
1 tablespoon lemon juice
¼ teaspoon salt
½ cup kirsch
Coloring

Stir softened gelatine in boiling water until dissolved. Add sugar, lemon juice, salt, kirsch, and coloring and stir well. Pour into a mold and chill. Unmold and serve with whipped cream. Serves 4.

Note: Yellow or red coloring can be used.

Little brown cookies
of chocolate and spice,
Smell awfully good,
And taste awfully nice!

LEMON ICE-BOX CAKE

1 envelope gelatine
1 cup sugar beaten with
  4 egg yolks
Rind of 1 lemon
Juice of 2 lemons
1 pint whipping cream
18 fresh lady fingers

Dissolve gelatine in 1/4 cup cold water. When dissolved, fill cup with warm water and stir thoroughly.

Add juice and lemon rind to beaten yolks, add gelatine mixture (no longer warm), fold in stiffly beaten whites, then stiffly whipped cream. Pour into spring form

33

which has been lined with halves of lady fingers, the rounded sides turned out, the round bottoms cut off straight. In lining bottom and sides, fill up all holes with pieces of lady fingers, to prevent seepage of lemon mixture.

Make crumbs from remaining lady fingers, brown lightly under flame in oven and sprinkle over top. Place in refrigerator. Before serving remove sides of pan, leaving bottom of pan under cake. Serves 12 generously.

LEMON MERINGUE PIE

1¼ cups sugar
5 tablespoons flour
4 eggs, separated
Pinch of salt
2 tablespoons butter
¾ cup strained lemon juice
1¼ cups boiling water
1 pie shell, baked

Bake pie shell. Mix 1 cup sugar, flour, egg yolks, salt, and butter. Add the lemon juice and boiling water, and cook in the top of a double boiler until thick, stirring almost constantly. Pour into baked pie shell.

Beat the 4 egg whites as stiff as possible, add ¼ cup sugar, and beat again. Spread the meringue on the pie so that it completely covers the filling, and bake until nicely brown (5 to 10 minutes) in a moderate oven, 350°. Cool slowly.

LEMON CHIFFON PIE

1 envelope gelatine, softened in
  ¼ cup cold water
½ cup lemon juice
1 cup sugar
4 eggs, separated
1 pie shell, baked

Soak gelatine in cold water for 5 minutes. Add lemon juice, ½ cup sugar, and beaten egg yolks. Cook in double boiler until slightly thickened, stirring constantly. Cool in refrigerator.

Beat egg whites until stiff; add ½ cup sugar. When lemon mixture begins to thicken (it should be somewhat rubbery), add it to the beaten egg whites. Beat with egg beater until thoroughly mixed and frothy. Pour into baked pie shell and cool.

Spread with a thin layer of whipped cream just before serving.

Macaroon Mousse,
Or Macaroon Mold;
Both taste of almond—
Serve them up cold!

MOCHA MOUSSE

8 ounces chocolate bits
3 tablespoons hot coffee
⅔ cup butter
6 eggs, separated
½ cup cream
5 tablespoons sugar

Melt the chocolate in the top of a double boiler, adding hot coffee. Add the butter and stir. Beat the egg yolks until very light and lemon-colored, and stir into the melted chocolate and butter. Cool. Whip the cream and add the sugar. Beat the egg whites until stiff but not dry. Fold in the cream and the egg whites. Refrigerate until ready to serve. Serves 6.

esselrode Chiffon's
The pie of all pies;
Sprinked with chocolate
It's a feast for sore eyes!

NESSELRODE CHIFFON PIE

1½ tablespoons plain gelatine
¼ cup cold water
1 cup milk
3 eggs, separated
1 cup light cream
¼ cup sugar or corn syrup
½ teaspoon salt
2 teaspoons vanilla
⅓ cup sugar
2 tablespoons chopped maraschino
    cherries
9-inch baked pie shell
2 tablespoons shaved sweet chocolate

Soften gelatine in cold water for 5 minutes. Scald milk and cream. Beat egg yolks slightly and add ¼ cup sugar or corn syrup and salt. Slowly add scalded milk and cream to egg mixture, stirring constantly. Cook over hot water, stirring constantly until mixture coats a spoon, about 7 minutes. Remove from heat. Add gelatine and stir until dissolved. Cool and add vanilla. Refrigerate until consistency of soft custard.

Beat egg whites until stiff, and fold in remaining sugar. Fold into gelatine mixture with cherries. Turn into pie shell. Sprinkle with chocolate. Chill.

NUT CAKE, À L'ORANGE

1 cup butter
1 cup sugar
3 eggs, separated
¾ cup sour cream
1 cup chopped nuts
Rind of orange and lemon
2 cups flour
Pinch of salt
1 teaspoon baking powder
1 teaspoon baking soda
½ cup sugar
Juice of orange and lemon

Cream sugar and butter, add egg yolks.

Alternate sour cream and flour mixture (flour with powder, soda, and salt) and add rind of lemon and orange, and nuts; lastly, fold in stiffly beaten egg whites. Bake in 325° oven for 1 hour — preferably in ring form. When cake is removed from oven, leave cake in pan. Place in cake rack.

Dissolve ½ cup of sugar with juice of orange and lemon and pour over hot cake. Leave in cake pan until liquid is absorbed.

NELLIE'S MOCK CHEESECAKE

4 eggs, separated
1 can sweet condensed milk
⅓ cup lemon juice, strained
1 teaspoon baking powder
1 teaspoon vanilla

Mix the milk, lemon juice, baking powder, vanilla, and yolks of the eggs. When well mixed, fold in stiffly beaten egg whites and bake in a 350° oven for about 40 minutes or until light brown.

This can also be made in a graham-cracker crust.

*ranges, lemons,
and pineapples too,
are cool and refreshing,
and so good for you!*

OUR FAVORITE
MAPLE MOUSSE

1 pint heavy cream, whipped
3 egg yolks
½ pint maple syrup

Beat egg yolks until light and lemon-colored, and combine with maple syrup in top of double boiler. Heat until mixture is thick enough to coat spoon. This may take some patience, but be sure that mixture is thick enough. Cool, and fold into whipped cream. Freeze in freezing compartment of refrigerator in covered pan. Let stand at least 4 hours or preferably overnight, without stirring. Serves 8.

40

*Pineapple Mousse
Is a holiday treat;
Lovely to look at,
and yummy to eat!*

PEACHES STUFFED WITH ALMONDS

12 halves fresh or canned peaches
1 tablespoon chopped glazed orange
  peel or citron
2 ounces shelled toasted almonds
3 ounces powdered sugar
¾ cup dry sherry

Peel, pit, and halve peaches. Chop almonds until mealy; add half the sugar; mix thoroughly. Add orange peel; blend. Then fill peach halves. Place in baking pan. Sprinkle with balance of sugar; pour in sherry. Bake in moderate oven 10 minutes. Serve warm. Serves 6.

PEARS IN WINE

4 pears
1 cup granulated sugar
1 cup water
4 whole cloves
1 cup port wine

Core pears from blossom end, leaving stems on. Simmer together sugar and water until sugar dissolves. Pare pears. Gently simmer pears, covered, in sugar syrup with cloves and wine about 30 minutes, or until tender. Refrigerate until well chilled. Remove cloves and serve.

PEARS MARY GARDEN

4 table pears
1 cup sugar
1 cup water
½ cup raspberry jam
1 teaspoon cornstarch
1 tablespoon kirsch
¼ cup candied cherries
½ cup whipped cream

Peel pears, cut in half and core. Boil sugar and water 3 minutes, stirring till sugar is dissolved. Add pears, lower heat and simmer till pears are tender. Cool pears in syrup and then drain well. Heat jam, stirring till softened; strain. Mix cornstarch with one tablespoon of water, add to strained jam and bring to a boil.

Cool, and add kirsch. Pour warm water over cherries and let stand till soft. Drain and dry. Add to jam. To serve, turn raspberry-cherry sauce into a serving dish, arrange cooled pears over sauce and garnish with whipped cream. Serves 4.

PUMPKIN PIE

1¼ cups pumpkin, cooked and strained
⅔ cup sugar
½ teaspoon salt
½ teaspoon ginger
1 teaspoon cinnamon
¼ teaspoon nutmeg
3 eggs, separated
1¼ cups scalded milk
1 six-ounce can (¾ cup) evaporated milk
½ recipe pastry

Thoroughly combine pumpkin, sugar, salt, and spices. Add egg yolks, milk, and blend. Fold in beaten egg whites. Pour into 9-inch pastry-lined pie pan. Bake in hot oven, 450°, 10 minutes, then in moderate oven, 325°, about 45 minutes, or until mixture does not stick to knife.

uite à la mode
Is a Chocolate Soufflé;
"our hostess is chic!"
Your friends will all say!

QUEEN MARIE'S MACAROON CREAM

1 dozen almond macaroons
½ pint cream, whipped
Sherry wine

Soak macaroons in sherry. Whip cream with 2 tablespoons fine sugar. Place some of macaroons on the bottom of a shallow bowl. Cover with cream, put more macaroons on top. Make 2 or 3 layers, finishing with macaroons soaked in sherry. Place in refrigerator and chill before serving. Serves 6.

A dessert to the queen's taste!

44

ed Devil's Food
Is my favorite cake;
serve it some time
after salad and steak!

RUM-FLAVORED
BAVARIAN CREAM

5 egg yolks
5 teaspoons granulated sugar
Rum to taste
½ pint sweet cream, whipped
1 dozen lady fingers

Beat together yolks and sugar until light
and creamy. Add rum to taste, and ½ pint
cream, whipped stiff. Cut lady fingers in
half lengthwise and line bowl. Pour in
half the mixture, cover with a layer of
lady fingers, and then with the remaining
cream mixture. Chill in refrigerator for
an hour or two before serving. Serves 6.

ROYAL COCOANUT CREAM PIE

1 cup milk
1⅓ cups sugar
Pinch of salt
2 egg yolks, beaten
2 tablespoons cornstarch
1 tablespoon milk
2½ teaspoons gelatine, dissolved in
  1 tablespoon milk
½ cup cocoanut
1 cup cream, whipped
1 teaspoon vanilla
2 egg whites, beaten
1 baked 10-inch pastry shell

Combine milk, sugar, and salt in saucepan and bring to a boil. Blend cornstarch and the milk and mix with yolks of eggs. Add to hot milk above and cook slightly. Dissolve gelatine in 1 tablespoon milk and pour hot mixture over it. Let set until firm. Put in electric beater and beat well.

Add cocoanut, whipped cream, and vanilla to above mixture and put in refrigerator for 10 minutes. Fold in stiffly beaten egg whites; pour in baked pastry shell; cover with whipped cream and sprinkle with cocoanut.

46

RICE, IMPERIALE

3 cups milk
½ cup rice (Minute Rice preferred)
2 tablespoons gelatine
¾ cup cold water
2 cups cream, whipped and flavored with
  a pinch of mace, 2 beaten egg whites,
  and sugar to taste
1 teaspoon vanilla
1 teaspoon almond extract

Pour milk into top of double boiler, and when boiling, stir in rice and a pinch of salt. Cook about 1½ hours, until tender and milk is nearly all boiled away.

Soak gelatine in cold water 1 hour; dissolve over hot water, and mix in the rice. Cool mixture; stir in vanilla and almond.

When rice mixture begins to set, stir in whipped cream to which a pinch of mace and 2 beaten egg whites have been added. Turn into a wet mold, and cool for an hour. Refrigerate overnight.

Sauce

Pour the juice off 1 can Bing Cherries; thicken with 2 tablespoons flour. Cool and add 2 tablespoons sugar, 2 tablespoons brandy and cherries. Serve over rice mold.

trawberries, sugared
and covered with cream,
Then cooled in the ice-box—
my mid-summer's dream!

STRAWBERRIES À LA TSARINA

3 cups stemmed strawberries
3 tablespoons powdered sugar
3 tablespoons port wine
3 tablespoons orange curaçao
3 tablespoons cognac
1 teaspoon curaçao
1 cup cream, whipped

Chill strawberries, tossed with sugar.

Blend port wine, orange curaçao and cognac and pour over berries. Add 1 teaspoon curaçao to whipped cream. Place berries in individual dishes, cover with whipped cream and serve. Serves 4.

48

STRAWBERRY ICE-BOX CAKE

2 envelopes gelatine
½ cup cold water
2 cups strawberries, sliced fine
  before measuring
1 cup sugar
1 cup hot water
4 teaspoons lemon juice
½ teaspoon salt
4 egg whites
½ cup sugar
1 cup cream, whipped
Lady fingers or sponge cake

Mix berries and 1 cup sugar together and let stand 5-10 minutes, stirring several times to draw out juice. Soften gelatine in cold water and dissolve in hot water. Add dissolved gelatine, lemon juice and salt to berries and stir well.

Cool, and when mixture begins to thicken fold in stiffly beaten egg whites to which ½ cup sugar has been added, and whipped cream. Line sides and bottom of spring form with sponge cake or lady fingers. Pour in filling, and top with sponge cake or lady fingers.

Chill in refrigerator. When firm, unmold

and garnish with whipped cream, slightly sweetened and flavored with vanilla; and strawberries. Serve 8-10.

SPANISH CREAM

½ cup sugar
1 envelope unflavored gelatine
Pinch of salt
2½ cups scalded milk
3 egg yolks, slightly beaten
1 teaspoon vanilla
3 egg whites, stiffly beaten

Combine sugar and gelatine in top of double boiler. Mix well. Add scalded milk and salt to the above mixture. Cook directly over medium heat, stirring until gelatine dissolves. Remove from heat.

Slowly stir slightly beaten egg yolks into the hot milk mixture. Return to top of double boiler and cook over hot water until mixture coats a metal spoon.

Add vanilla. Fold hot custard mixture very gradually into beaten egg whites. Pour into mold. Chill until firm. Serve with whipped cream. Serves 6-8.

For rum flavor, substitute 2 tablespoons Jamaica Rum for the vanilla.

SPONGE CAKE

6 eggs, separated
1 cup sugar
1 teaspoon lemon juice
Rind of 1 lemon
1 cup cake flour
½ teaspoon baking powder
¼ teaspoon salt

Beat the egg yolks until lemon-colored and light, adding sugar little by little as you beat. Add lemon juice and rind, and cake flour which has been sifted twice with baking powder and salt. Beat egg whites until stiff but not dry and fold in.

Bake in tubular pan, which has been rubbed with flour, in a 325° oven for 45 minutes. Turn over onto a cake rack, inverting cake. Do not remove from pan until thoroughly cool.

SOUFFLÉ GRAND MARNIER

9 eggs
⅔ cup Grand Marnier
3 tablespoons powdered sugar
1 cup cream, whipped

Separate the eggs. Combine the yolks with the Grand Marnier and sugar and beat well until thick. Beat the whites very stiff and fold into the yolk mixture. Pour into a buttered soufflé dish. Bake in a 375° oven approximately 30-40 minutes. When the soufflé breaks away from the edge of the dish, it should be served immediately with whipped cream. Serves 4.

SURPRISE PIE

32 graham crackers
Butter
1 tablespoon gelatine (1 pkg.)
1 cup milk
2 eggs, separated
1 cup sugar
1 pint heavy cream, whipped
2 teaspoons vanilla or rum

Line 2 nine-inch pie tins with graham crackers and butter, mixed, saving out some for top.

Dissolve gelatine in milk and heat until warm. Beat egg yolks with sugar. Slowly add milk to sugar and eggs. Return to double boiler and cook for seven minutes. When cool, fold in egg whites, beaten, and whipped cream. Add vanilla (or rum). Sprinkle remaining crumbs on top. Chill in refrigerator 8-24 hours.

ortes from Vienna,
Frothy and light,
are wonderfully tasty—
a gourmet's delight!

TROPICAL CHEESE TARTS

Pastry
4 eggs
½ cup sugar
⅛ teaspoon salt
1 cup milk
1 teaspoon vanilla
1 cup fine cottage cheese
1 cup flaked cocoanut

Line 3-inch tart pans with pastry. Beat eggs in top of double boiler. Add sugar, salt, milk. Place over boiling water, and cook, until thickened, stirring constantly.

Remove from heat, and add vanilla. Fold

in cheese and cocoanut; pour into prepared pans. Bake in hot oven, at 425°, for
15 to 18 minutes, or until done. Makes 12
tarts.

*This is a dessert that is reminiscent of the
islands of the South Seas!*

TARTES À L'ABRICOT

3 tablespoons flour
1/4 teaspoon salt
1/4 teaspoon cloves
1/2 teaspoon nutmeg
1 cup sugar
1 cup sour cream
3 eggs, beaten
1 1/2 cups cooked apricots
Pastry

Fit rich pastry into 8 deep muffin pans to
make tart shells. Mix flour with salt, spices
and sugar. Add cream, eggs and apricots.
Fill tarts and bake 10 minutes in moderate oven. Lower heat and bake 25 minutes. Let tarts remain 10 minutes in pans
to cool and then carefully slip them out,
using fork and spatula.

*A Viennese twist to a favorite French des-
sert!*

TORTA DI RICOTTA

2 cups flour
1 teaspoon baking powder
1/4 teaspoon salt
3/4 cup soft butter
2 tablespoons cognac
1 1/2 pounds ricotta (Italian pot cheese)
2 tablespoons chopped almonds
3 tablespoons toasted pine nuts
2 tablespoons chopped citron
4 eggs
1 cup sugar
1 1/2 teaspoons vanilla
Confectioners' sugar

Mix 2 cups sifted flour, baking powder, and salt. Work in butter. Gradually add cognac, mixing lightly just until dough holds together. Chill. Then roll about 2/3 of dough 1/8 inch thick and line 10-inch pie pan. Mix 1 tablespoon flour, cheese, nuts, and citron. Beat eggs until light and lemon-colored. Gradually beat in sugar; add vanilla. Stir into cheese mixture. Pour into lined pie pan. Roll remaining pastry to 1/8-inch thickness, and cut in strips. Arrange, lattice-fashion, on pie. Bake in 375° oven 40 minutes, or until firm. Cool. Just before serving, sift confectioners' sugar lightly on top.

Under the shade
of an old apple tree,
Let's nibble our cookies,
and sip our iced-tea!

UNEEDA BISCUIT CAKE

6 eggs, separated
1 cup sugar
8 Uneeda biscuits
½ ounce brandy
1 teaspoon baking powder
½ cup grated walnuts
¼ teaspoon each: cinnamon, cloves, nutmeg

Beat 6 egg yolks with 1 cup of sugar. Add 8 Uneeda biscuits, rolled fine, then the brandy. Add 1 teaspoon baking powder, ½ cup grated walnuts, and the spices. Add egg whites, well beaten. Bake in two layers. Fill and top with whipped cream and grated walnuts.

56

Vienna's the city
For pastry divine—
Save room for dessert,
Though you heavily dine!

VIENNA SACHER TORTE

¾ cup butter
6 ounces semi-sweet chocolate
¾ cup sugar
8 egg yolks
1 cup flour
10 egg whites, stiffly beaten
2 tablespoons apricot jam

Beat butter until creamy. Melt chocolate.
Add sugar and chocolate to butter; stir.
Add egg yolks one at a time. Add flour.
Fold in egg whites.

Grease and butter 9-inch cake tin. Pour
in mixture. Bake in 275° oven about 1
hour. Test with toothpick or straw. Re-

move to board; cool. Cut top off and turn bottom up. Split cake into 2 layers.

Heat apricot jam slightly and spread over top and between layers. Cover with chocolate icing, prepared as follows:

Chocolate Icing

1 cup sugar
⅓ cup water
7 ounces semi-sweet chocolate

Cook sugar and water to thin thread. Melt chocolate in top of double boiler. Add sugar gradually to chocolate. Stir constantly until icing coats the spoon. Pour on top of cake.

VINNY'S PEARS WITH GINGER

8 firm cooking pears
1 cup sugar
⅛ teaspoon powdered ginger
2 slices lemon

Peel pears, cut in half and remove cores. Drop into 2½ cups of boiling water, cover and simmer 10 minutes. Add sugar, ginger, lemon, then cover and cook till tender, 10 to 15 minutes. Cool. Serves 8.

VIENNESE MALAKOFF PUDDING

½ cup sweet butter
½ cup fine granulated sugar
1 medium-sized can fruit cup
Rum
½ cup blanched, finely chopped almonds
3 egg yolks
¼ teaspoon vanilla extract
1 pint heavy cream, scalded and cooled
Lady fingers

Cream butter, add sugar and blend well. Dip the well-drained fruit pieces into rum and add them one by one, stirring well before adding the next one. Add the almonds, the 3 egg yolks and ½ pint of cream (saving the other ½), 1 teaspoon at a time, stirring slowly until all the cream has been used.

Line a bowl with lady fingers; alternate 1 layer of the mixture with a layer of lady fingers which have been dipped into the remaining ½ pint of cream.

Put a cover, which is smaller than the bowl, on top of the bowl, something heavy over it to weigh it down, and set in the refrigerator for 24 hours.

*Whip up a pudding,
Whip up a froth;
We're having a party,
There's no time for sloth!*

WHITE MOUNTAIN

¼ cup bottled chestnuts in syrup,
   finely chopped
¼ cup syrup from chestnuts
2 tablespoons brandy
1 cup heavy cream, whipped

In bottom of each sherbet glass, combine 1 tablespoon chopped chestnuts, 1 tablespoon syrup, 1½ teaspoons brandy. Place in refrigerator until well chilled — about 2 hours.

To serve, top generously with whipped cream. Serves 4.

abagliones's the measure
of an elegant cook:
It ends a fine dinner;
It ends my fine book!

ZABAGLIONE

6 egg yolks
⅓ cup sugar
⅓ cup Marsala or Sherry

In the top of a double boiler, beat egg
yolks until thick, and add granulated
sugar, gradually. Keep beating with a ro-
tary beater until thick and foamy, being
careful that the water in the bottom of
the double boiler does not boil. In about
5 minutes, slowly add wine, beating until
thick. Heap into glass sherbets and serve
at once. Serves 4.

THIS VOLUME IS DESIGNED, PRINTED

AND PUBLISHED AT THE OFFICE OF

THE PETER PAUPER PRESS